797,885 Books
are available to read at

www.ForgottenBooks.com

Forgotten Books' App
Available for mobile, tablet & eReader

ISBN 978-1-333-27429-0
PIBN 10482417

This book is a reproduction of an important historical work. Forgotten Books uses state-of-the-art technology to digitally reconstruct the work, preserving the original format whilst repairing imperfections present in the aged copy. In rare cases, an imperfection in the original, such as a blemish or missing page, may be replicated in our edition. We do, however, repair the vast majority of imperfections successfully; any imperfections that remain are intentionally left to preserve the state of such historical works.

Forgotten Books is a registered trademark of FB &c Ltd.
Copyright © 2017 FB &c Ltd.
FB &c Ltd, Dalton House, 60 Windsor Avenue, London, SW19 2RR.
Company number 08720141. Registered in England and Wales.

For support please visit www.forgottenbooks.com

1 MONTH OF FREE READING

at

www.ForgottenBooks.com

By purchasing this book you are eligible for one month membership to ForgottenBooks.com, giving you unlimited access to our entire collection of over 700,000 titles via our web site and mobile apps.

To claim your free month visit:
www.forgottenbooks.com/free482417

* Offer is valid for 45 days from date of purchase. Terms and conditions apply.

English
Français
Deutsche
Italiano
Español
Português

www.forgottenbooks.com

Mythology Photography **Fiction** Fishing Christianity **Art** Cooking Essays Buddhism Freemasonry Medicine **Biology** Music **Ancient Egypt** Evolution Carpentry Physics Dance Geology **Mathematics** Fitness Shakespeare **Folklore** Yoga Marketing **Confidence** Immortality Biographies Poetry **Psychology** Witchcraft Electronics Chemistry History **Law** Accounting **Philosophy** Anthropology Alchemy Drama Quantum Mechanics Atheism Sexual Health **Ancient History Entrepreneurship** Languages Sport Paleontology Needlework Islam **Metaphysics** Investment Archaeology Parenting Statistics Criminology **Motivational**

PHILOLOGICAL SOCIETY.

TALMUDICAL AND RABBINICAL LITERATURE.

BY
DR. AD. NEUBAUER.

ASHER & CO.'S PUBLICATIONS.

ASHER, A.—THE ITINERARY OF RABBI BENJAMIN OF
Tudela. The Hebrew Text, with an English Translation. Two vols. 8vo. £1. 4s.

BOLTZ (DR. A.).—A NEW CONVERSATION GRAMMAR OF
the German Language, adapted to the use of Schools and Private Instruction, after the practical and theoretical method of Robertson. 3 parts in 1 vol., cloth, 8vo. 5s.

BRUENNOW (DR. F.).—SPHERICAL ASTRONOMY. Translated
by the Author from the second German edition. 8vo. cloth. 16s.

BUXTORFII LEXICON CHALDAICUM TALMUDICUM ET
Rabbinicum denuo editum et annotatis auctum. Parts 1 to 28. Imp. 8vo.
1s. 6d. each.

COHN (ALBERT).—SHAKESPEARE IN GERMANY IN THE
Sixteenth and Seventeenth Centuries. An account of English Actors in Germany and the Netherlands, and of the plays performed by them during the same Period. With 2 plates of Facsimiles. 4to. cloth. £1 8s.

DORANGE, CH.—PRACTICAL METHOD OF THE FRENCH
Language, containing Exercises, Letters, Stories accompanied by Questions, forming Conversations. Approved by His Excellency the Minister of Public Instruction in France. 2nd ed. 16mo. 2s.

EWALD'S (PROF. H.) INTRODUCTORY HEBREW GRAMMAR
for the Use of Beginners. Translated, with Special Improvements, from the German Edition, with the Author's concurrence, by the Rev. J. Fred. Smith. 8vo cloth. 6s.

FINDEL (T. G.)—HISTORY OF FREEMASONRY. 8vo. cloth. 12s.

GALERIE DES MARBRES ANTIQUES DU MUSÉE CAMPANA
à Rome. Sculptures Grecques et Romanes, avec une Introduction et un texte descriptif, par Henry D'Escamps. With 108 photographic Plates. Fol. 2nd ed. £9.

GESENIUS'S STUDENT'S HEBREW GRAMMAR; from the 20th
German Edition, as revised by E. Rödiger, D.D., Professor of Oriental Languages at the University of Berlin. Translated by B. Davies, LL.D. With special Additions and Improvements by Dr. Rödiger; and with Reading-Book and Exercises by the Translator. 8vo. cloth. 7s. 6d.

HOCHSTETTER, F.—NEW ZEALAND; its Physical Geography,
Geology, and Natural History. with Special Reference to the Results of Government Expeditions in the Provinces of Auckland and Nelson. Translated from the German Original by E. Sauter. With woodcuts, chromo-lithographs, and maps. Royal 8vo. £1 1s.

KEANE (A. H.).—THE TRUE THEORY OF GERMAN DECLENSION and Conjugation. 8vo. cloth. 2s. 6d.

LENORMANT'S STUDENT'S MANUAL OF ORIENTAL
History: a Manual of the Ancient History of the East to the Commencement of the Median Wars; comprising the History of the Israelites, Egyptians, Assyrians, Phœnicians, and Carthaginians, Babylonians, Medians, Persians, and Arabians. By François Lenormant, Librarian at the Institute of France. Translated from the Third revised Edition by E. Chevallier, Member of the Royal Asiatic Society. 2 vols. Post 8vo. cloth. 12s.

The Second Volume contains a Table of Semitic Alphabets, together with the Alphabet of Moabite Inscription of Mesha.

13, Bedford Street, Covent Garden, W.C.

TALMUDICAL AND RABBINICAL LITERATURE.

"Hebrew, modified in its grammatical forms and enriched by the introduction of words of other Semitic idioms, or even of Greek and Latin, is commonly called Rabbinic; it can scarcely be considered a dead language, for it is not only employed for books on all branches of science and literature, but is also spoken by a great number of Jews at the present time. Not only books relating to Hebraico-Rabbinical literature have been written in Rabbinic, but classical works of various nations, such as the tragedies of Racine, Shakspeare's Othello, Milton,[1] Lessing's Nathan the Wise, and even Goethe's Faust,[2] have been translated into it. The last-named work may, without doubt, be considered a great success; and the translator, the late Dr. Letteris, has in our judgment in many respects surpassed the original. The *dramatis personae* are taken from Jewish history; for instance, the learned and dissatisfied Faust is represented by the Talmudical Elishah, son of Abuyah, who, searching too deeply for the solution of theosophical problems, was finally driven to apostasy. Any Hebrew scholar will read the above-mentioned translations with as much pleasure as the Book of Job. A still better proof can be given of the truth of the assertion that Rabbinic is still a living language. Novels, both originals and translations, are yearly published in this idiom. The

---

[1] *Ittai hak-Kushi (the Cushite), Othello, der Mohr von Venedig,* translated from the English into Hebrew by J. E. Salkinson, with a critical introduction by P. Smolensky. 8vo. Vienna, 1874. *Milton's Paradise Lost, in Hebrew blank verse,* by J. E. S. (no date).

[2] *Ben Abuyah, Goethe's Faust, eine Tragoedie in einer hebräischen Umdichtung.* 8vo. Vienna, 1865.

late Mapo of Kowno (Poland) wrote, amongst several others, a novel under the title *The Love of Sion*,[1] which is a masterly production, both in style and matter. A description of Jewish life in Galicia has appeared in the monthly paper called *hash-Shahar*, which has been considered worthy of a translation into French for the *Révue des deux mondes*.[2] Sue's *Mystères de Paris*,[3] translated into Hebrew, has reached several editions. Finally, treatises on general and special historical subjects, on various branches of natural science, medicine, and mathematics, are constantly published in Rabbinic. These publications are read by Jews in the East, Poland and Russia, Hungary and the Danubian provinces, to whom the Hebrew language is much more accessible than that spoken in their respective countries. No less than four weekly papers are published in Hebrew,[4] the first columns of which are devoted to current politics, and the last to literature and advertisements. Of course these papers must be read by Jews who know only Rabbinic, or to whom it is more familiar than any other language. Let us also mention a well-known fact, viz. that many of the *beau sèxe* participate in the knowledge of this language. Who would venture after this to assert that the so-called Rabbinical idiom is a completely dead language? We have still to explain our assertion that it is spoken by many Jews. In Jerusalem, for instance, where the Jewish population is composed of men coming from Arabic-speaking countries, from Persia and Kurdistan, from Armenia and Turkey, from Greece and Poland, the only means of communication is Rabbinic, which they all speak more or less fluently. The *Alliance Israëlite* at Paris and Vienna, as well as the Anglo-Jewish Association in London, communicate with the Eastern Jews in Hebrew, and all casu-

---

[1] *Ahabath Cion*, amor Zionis, fabula romanensis, e tempore regis *Achas*. 8vo. Wilna, 1864.

[2] 15th of September, 1875.

[3] *Misteré Paris*. 8vo. Wilna, 1857. The Hebrew word *Misteré* means "hidden things."

[4] a. The *ham-Maggid*, published at Lyck (Prussia); b. The *hal-Lebanon*, at Mayence; c. The *haz-Zefirah*, at Warsaw; d. The *Habazeleth*, at Jerusalem. The *hak-Karmel*, at Wilna, is now a monthly magazine, and the *ham-Melitz*, at Odessa, has ceased with its tenth year of existence.

istical correspondence between the rabbis of various countries is carried on in that language. What an active communication is kept up among the learned Jews of all countries may be seen from the publication of several quarterlies,[1] as well as commentaries on the Bible and Talmud, written in this idiom. Strange it is that no attempt has yet been made to bring out a grammar and a lexicon of Rabbinic, so as to enable any one to acquire a fair knowledge of it without the assistance of a Jewish teacher. Biblical and Semitic scholars can scarcely do without an acquaintance with this strange idiom, since important articles on biblical criticism, as well as on inscriptions of various kinds, are to be found in modern Rabbinical publications. We are glad to state that there is a school at Oxford and Cambridge which begins to cultivate this idiom, as will be seen from the various publications made by younger members of both Universities.

"After this introduction on the present state of Rabbinic, we shall pass on to the enumeration of the various publications issued in different countries during the last ten years, having first accounted for the omissions which any critic may easily discover in this report. Scattered as the Jewish people is all over the world, so scattered are their literary productions in various periodicals, as the following considerations will show. 1. Rabbinical learning being concerned with various branches of science and literature, the specialist may expect to find his own particular subject treated, not in periodicals of general Rabbinic literature, but in publications devoted to his specialty. We must therefore not be astonished to find Dr. Steinschneider publishing papers on the history of mathematics and medicine in Schlömlich's[2] and Virchow's[3] *Zeitschriften;* on matters

---

[1] The *he-Haluz,* published by *S*chorr; the *Yeshurun,* by Kobak; the *Kokhbe Yizhaq,* by *S*tern and Weiss; the *hash-Shahar,* by *S*molensky; the *hak-Karmel,* by Finn; the *Or Thorah,* by Kohen Zedeq.

[2] *Abraham Judaeus and Zum Speculum astronomicum des Albertus Magnus,* etc., Zeitschrift für Mathematik und Physik, tomes xii. and xiv.

[3] *Constantinus Africanus ; Donolo; die toxologischen Schriften der Araber bis Ende des xii. Jahrhunderts,* Archiv für pathologische Anatomie, etc. Tomes xxxvii. xxxviii. and lii.

concerning the Romance languages in Lemcke's *Jahrbuch*.[1] This last subject is also treated by M. Darmesteter, of Paris, in the *Romania*,[2] and by Professor Böhmer and the writer of this report in the *Romanische Studien*.[3] Historical subjects on the Khazars and Sclaves are published in Russian periodicals by Dr. Harkavy,[4] on Italy by Signor Lattes in the *Archivio Veneto*,[5] on French rabbis by M. Renan together with the present writer in the *Histoire littéraire de la France*,[6] and by M. Adrien de Longpérier in the *Journal des Savants*.[7] Rabbinic, being a step-daughter of Hebrew, has also a right to be considered a branch of an Oriental language, and so we may expect to find papers on it in periodicals devoted to those studies. Thus Dr. Zunz, the late Dr. Geiger, as well as Dr. Steinschneider and others, have contributed papers on Rabbinical philology in the *Deutsch-morgenländische Zeitschrift*; M. Derenbourg and the writer of this report have done the same in the *Journal Asiatique*; Professors F. Lasinio, De Benedetti, and Castelli, as well as Abbate Perreau in the *Annuario*;[8] the Rev. Dr. Schiller-Szinessy in the Transactions of the Biblical-Archaeological Society.[9] 2. The savants belonging to various countries contribute to the publications of the academies of their own countries. We shall have to mention by and by many of these important publications. 3. Matters exclusively concerning Rabbinical literature find their place in special periodicals edited by Jewish savants in Hebrew or German. We have already mentioned the former; the most important of the latter are those edited by Drs.

---

[1] *Ysopet hebräisch, ein Beitrag zur Geschichte der Fabeln im Mittelalter*, Jahrbuch für romanische, etc., Literatur, t. xiii. p. 351.

[2] *Glosses et glossaires hébreux-français au moyen-âge*, Romania, t. ii. p. 146; *deux élégies du Vatican*, ibid. iii. p. 443.

[3] *Un vocabulaire hébraico-français*, Romanische Studien, t. i. p. 103; *de vocabulis franco-gallicis Judaice transcriptis*, ibid. p. 197.

[4] *Transactions of the Archaeological Society* (in Russian), 1872 to 1874.

[5] Tomes v. vi. and vii.   [6] Tome xxvii. p. 431 seqq.

[7] *Inscriptions de la France, du v⁵ siècle au xviii⁵*, etc. Journal des Savants, 1874, p. 647 seqq.

[8] *Annuario della società italiana per gli studii orientali*, Firenze, 1873-74.

[9] *Transactions of the Society for Biblical Archaeology*, 1872, pp. 263-270.

Geiger,[1] Steinschneider[2] and Berliner,[3] at Berlin, and by Professor Graetz at Breslau.[4] Dr. N. Brüll also edits an annuaire,[5] and Dr. Rahmer a literary fortnightly appendix to a Jewish periodical.[6] The periodical edited by Dr. Philippson[7] has also from time to time small literary articles. Let us in addition mention the *Révue Israëlite* in Paris, which only existed for a year, and the *Israelitische Letterbode* edited at Amsterdam by M. Roest. Other Jewish periodicals, written in French, Italian, and English, must be passed over in silence, as possessing no literary importance. With this vast number of papers published in various languages every year on Rabbinical subjects, it is certainly impossible not to be guilty of omissions in a report extending over ten years. It may be added too that many of the articles are either mere notes or of too little importance to be worthy of special notice. So much for the omission of articles published in periodicals. As regards books, too, we can be no more complete. Russia, Poland, Hungary, various Eastern towns, and Leghorn produce every year a large quantity of Rabbinical literature on various subjects : Biblical and Talmudical commentaries, books of prayers and casuistry, Kabbalistical and legendary works, modern poetry, general history, and treatises on natural science, besides new editions of old publications without any help from MSS. ; most of these publications never reach our libraries, and we shall not be too severe if we say that we are not any the worse for it. Not to know them may be a loss bibliographically, but not for literature. We shall therefore have nothing to show from those countries if we only except the works of Reifmann, Gottlober, and Gurland.

"Let us now come to the most important publications of

---

[1] *Jüdische Zeitschrift für Wissenschaft und Leben*, 1862 to 1875, ceased to appear in consequence of the Editor's death.
[2] *Ham-Mazkir, hebräische Bibliographie*, 1858, seqq.
[3] *Magazin für jüdische Literatur*, 1874 and 1875.
[4] *Monatsschrift für Geschichte und Wissenschaft des Judenthums*, begun by the late Dr. Frankel in 1845.
[5] *Jahrbücher für jüdische Geschichte und Literatur*, 1874.
[6] *Beilage zur jüdischen Wochenschrift*, 1870 seqq.
[7] *Allgemeine Zeitung des Judenthums*, 1838 seqq.

the last decennium, and, in order to be as methodical as possible, let us begin with *a.* books and monographs containing descriptions of libraries, both public and private, of printed books and MSS.; next will follow *b.* an enumeration of the most important contributions to Talmudical writings; *c.* of commentaries on the Holy Scriptures; *d.* of grammatical and lexicographical works; *e.* of poetry; *f.* of philosophical and miscellaneous texts. Karaitic and Samaritan literature are subjects too closely connected with Rabbinic to be omitted here; a brief account of them will therefore follow as a kind of appendix.

"CATALOGUES.—The Library of the British Museum possesses, no doubt, after the Bodleian, the best collection of printed Rabbinical books, the catalogue of which, made by the late Mr. Zedner, has been published by order of the Trustees.[1] The late L. Rosenthal, a very learned Jew of Hanover, possessed one of the best collections of Rabbinical books to be found; it is now at Amsterdam, in the possession of his son George; the catalogue of it has been published on the model of that of the British Museum by M. Roest,[2] the editor of the *Israelitische Letterbode*. The much regretted Solomon Munk, member of the Institut de France, and Professor of Hebrew in the Collège de France, was, during his tenure of office in the National Library of Paris, preparing the catalogue of its Hebrew MSS. This is undoubtedly the best collection of Rabbinical MSS. after those of the Bodleian Library and the British Museum. He having lost the use of his eyes in 1848, M. J. Derenbourg, now member of the Institut de France, was engaged to revise his slips and to describe the MSS. left uncatalogued by Munk. Through some difficulties connected with the administration of the library, M. Derenbourg did not publish this result of the labours of Munk and himself; a second revision was then made by M. Franck, member of the Institut and Professor in the Collège de France, who, being mostly interested in

---

[1] *Catalogue of the Hebrew Books in the Library of the British Museum*, 1867.
[2] *Catalog der Hebraica und Judaica aus der L. Rosenthal'schen Bibliothek.* 2 vols. Amsterdam, 1875.

the history of the Kabbalah, paid full attention only to the MSS. belonging to that branch of literature. Finally, M. Zotenberg, who, though a born Jew, is not a Rabbinical scholar, revised the already twice revised slips, and spoiled the labour of his predecessors by shortening them, and by his inability to fill up the gaps left by Munk and Derenbourg. We may apply here the proverb, 'too many cooks spoil the broth;' but in spite of its faults, he has brought out a useful catalogue, with a carefully elaborated index.[1] The Royal Library of Munich, although not one of the richest in Hebrew MSS., as far as quantity is concerned (there are only 418), has a well-selected set of works, and many of their MSS. have been published in this century. We shall have to mention amongst Talmudical publications the complete MS. of the Talmud of Babylon existing in this Library. Dr. Lilienthal published in 1838 and 1839 a short description of this collection, but at that time the knowledge of Rabbinical literature was not advanced enough to enable him to describe such an important collection correctly, and the author was, we must say, a very poor scholar even for his time. It is indeed fortunate for Rabbinical literature that the well-known bibliographer Dr. Steinschneider undertook to make a catalogue of this collection.[2] The author is here perhaps a little too short, certainly much shorter than in his catalogues of the printed books in the Bodleian Library and of the MSS. in the Library of Leyden. He is, we are glad to state, not so aggressive against others as in his former works, and this catalogue has the advantage of being written in German, whilst the others are composed in a very unintelligible Latin.—Russia is a rival of other great states, not only politically, but also in literary activity—a rivalry of the greatest advantage for the progress of science and literature. Her academies and other societies are doing, if not more, at least as much as those of Paris, Berlin, and Vienna. Its

---

[1] *Catalogues des Manuscrits hébreux et samaritains de la bibliothèque Impériale*, Paris, 1866.

[2] *Die hebräischen Handschriften der K. Hof- und Staatsbibliothek in München*, 1875.

memoirs and books on philology and archaeology were formerly published in French and German; they begin now to appear in Russian, which, although inconvenient for most non-Russian savants, is in our opinion thoroughly right. We shall have to learn Russian as we were obliged to learn French and German. The St. Petersburg collections of MSS. of all languages had long been of equal importance to those of the richest libraries of Europe; the Hebrew MSS. alone were of inferior value until 1860, when the Emperor bought a collection of more than 1000 MSS., collected from various synagogues and private libraries in the Crimea as well as in the East, by the late learned Karaite Abraham Firkovitz. Through this acquisition the Imperial Library of St. Petersburg is at present the richest in the world in old Biblical MSS. and works in Karaitic literature; in the latter department it is absolutely unrivalled. The writer of the present notice has given a short account in French and German of the most important of them.[1] We understand that the Russian Government is going to purchase a still richer collection made somewhat later by the same A. Firkovitz. This collection of about 1000 MSS. will add much to the former in Biblical MSS., and by the possession of it the St. Petersburg Library will out-rival the Bodleian Library, which up to this time has been the first for Jewish-Arabic literature. It would be superfluous to say what a boon to the students of Rabbinical literature the publication of the catalogue of the St. Petersburg collection will be. A beginning has been already made; we have before us the first part of this catalogue, comprising the Biblical MSS., by Drs. Harkavy and Strack.[2] No better choice of editors could have been made for such an important collection.—As to our own country, whose three great libraries, viz. the British Museum, the Bodleian Library at Oxford, and the University Library of Cambridge, count above 4000 MSS., we are happy to state that no less

---

[1] *Jour. Asiatique*, 1865, t. v. p. 539 seqq. ; *aus der Petersburger Bibliothek.* Leipzig, 1866.
[2] *Catalog der hebräischen Bibelhandschriften der Kaiserlichen öffentlichen Bibliothek in St. Petersburg, erster und zweiter Theil*, 1875.

activity is displayed here. Dr. Schiller-Szinessy has just brought out the first volume of his most minute catalogue of the MSS. of the University Library of Cambridge, comprising seventy-two numbers, viz. the Biblical MSS., the commentaries on the Holy Scriptures and the super-commentaries.[1] About six years ago be assisted Mr. Aldis Wright in cataloguing the small collection of Hebrew MSS. belonging to Trinity College, Cambridge. The catalogue too of more than 2000 numbers of the Bodleian collection is already printed off, and only about 500 more remain to be printed, and it is to be hoped that the work will be completed by this time next year. Let us also mention the brief but somewhat insufficient description of the small collection of the Hebrew MSS. belonging to Christ Church, Oxford. We trust that a description of the Hebrew MSS. scattered throughout the various colleges of Oxford will be added as an appendix to the Bodleian Catalogue. As to the British Museum, which possesses, we believe, nearly 750 Hebrew MSS., we understand that the Trustees will provide for their being catalogued as soon as Dr. Wright's Catalogue of the Ethiopic MSS. shall have left the press, which, as far as we know, will be the case at the end of the present year. Finally, Dr. Zuckermann has brought out the first part of the Catalogue of the works belonging to the Library of the Rabbinical School at Breslau, comprising the MSS. and the printed Bibles.[2] Before leaving the great public libraries, we have to mention minor descriptions of some other libraries. The present writer was sent by the French Government in 1868 to examine the Hebrew MSS. of Spain and Portugal. There are not more than 100 now left in those countries, the seat of Hebrew learning of all branches during a period of five centuries (1040 to 1490). In 1872 and 1873 he was sent to do the same in other public libraries of France, and especially to search in Italian and German libraries for the works of French rabbis. A

---

[1] *Catalogue of Hebrew MSS. preserved in the University Library, Cambridge.* vol. i. 1876.
[2] *Jahresbericht*, 1870.

summary account of them was given by the writer to the Minister of Public Instruction in Paris.[1] In their commentaries, both on the Holy Scriptures as well as on the Talmud, these rabbis, in order to explain difficult words, often give a translation of them in the vernacular, viz. in French and Provençal, and this is a matter of the highest importance for the history of those dialects from the twelfth to the fourteenth century. The famous R. Salomon Isaaki of Troyes, known better under the name of Rashi, has alone in his commentaries more than 2000 words. This Rabbi having written as early as the eleventh century, a period to which few documents written in the dialect of Champagne belong, his glosses are of the highest importance. Their value is still more enhanced by their being written in Hebrew characters, and very often provided with vowel-points, and we are thus enabled to fix the pronunciation of many old French words in the eleventh century. This branch of study has been taken up by M. A. Darmesteter in Paris, who was also sent out by the French Government to England and to Parma for the purpose of collating those glosses with other MSS. In his report to the Minister of Public Instruction M. Darmesteter had necessarily to give a description of the numerous MSS. he had examined.[2] We owe also some valuable accounts of MSS. in Italian libraries to Dr. Berliner, who, assisted by the Prussian Government, devoted the year 1872 to the examination of Hebrew MSS. at Rome, Parma, Florence, Milan, and some minor places.[3] Finally, the Abbate Perreau, Sub-Librarian of the Library at Parma, has described MSS. of that library, chiefly those added to the rich collection of De-Rossi.[4] We have to deplore the loss of two eminent Jewish scholars in Italy, viz. the well-known S. D. Luzzatto and Lelio Della Torre, both professors at the Rabbinical school of Padua; both had important libraries, that of the former being especially rich in MSS. Short catalogues of these collections, as well as of another belonging to the well-known

---

[1] *Archives des missions scientifiques*, 1868 and 1873.   [2] Ibidem 1874 and 1876.
[3] See his *Magazin*, 1874 and 1875.   [4] *Ham-Mazkir*, 1870 seqq.

bibliographer M. Ghirondi, have been published. Another has been published of the library of the late D. Cardoso of Amsterdam, which was chiefly remarkable for its Hebraico-Spanish printed and MSS. works; and also of a small collection of MSS. in the possession of the booksellers Benzian at Berlin, and Fischl Hirsch at Halberstadt. Finally, in November last the important library of the late D. Carmoly was in the market, the short catalogue of which is of some value. This, we think, is all of importance relating to libraries.

"TALMUD.—The vast encyclopaedical work comprising the teaching of the schools of Palestine and Babylonia from 150 B.C. to 700 A.D. is called by the name of Talmud, which means in our language 'the result of teaching.' In one word, it contains the post-biblical literature of the Rabbis, for nothing is extant in Hebrew between the latest biblical book and the Talmud. The apocryphal writings, a great number of which were composed in the post-biblical Hebrew dialect, not having been admitted into the Canon by the Rabbinical schools, have reached us in the shape of translations only. Although the origin, development, and various divisions of the Talmud have been made known to the English public by the able popular article of the late Mr. Deutsch, we must mention the names of the various works of which it consists before we proceed to enumerate the critical editions of them which have appeared in the course of the last decennium. It consists of the Mishnah, the Tosiftha, the Gemara of Jerusalem and of Babylon, the Siphrâ, the Siphré, the Mekhiltha, the Pesiqtha, and the various books of the Midrash. The Mishnah, which is the oldest of the Talmudical books, and composed in concise sentences, is written in a Hebrew which is relatively pure, excepting certain technical expressions borrowed from other Semitic dialects, or from Greek and Latin. All parts of it are of a ritual character, except that called *Abhoth*, or sayings of the fathers, which is an ethical treatise. It has been translated into various languages from the *textus receptus*, which unfortunately offers many doubtful readings. Dr. Cahn has begun a critical edition of it, as it was read by old commentators, of whom the most important is the famous Maimonides, adding to it a German commentary, in which the philological element is most prominent.[1] It is to be regretted that the editor had no opportunity of visiting the Libraries of Oxford and Cambridge, which possess a great number of old MSS. of the text of Abhoth, and also commentaries in which the readings of very old MSS. are quoted. We hope that the Rev. C. Taylor, Fellow of St. John's College, Cambridge, who is preparing an edition of this text, together with a later ethical book called 'Abhoth according to R. Nathan,' will supply this deficiency in Dr. Cahn's edition. Two important works in Hebrew have appeared on the method of the Mishnah, and on the history of the doctors whose sayings on ethics and ritual are mentioned in it: the one by the late Dr. Frankel, Director of the Rabbinical School of Breslau,[2] and the other by the Rabbi J. Brüll.[3] We may add that the literary history of the Jews, from the time of the building of the second Temple to that of the composition of the Mishnah, by J. Weiss,[4] treats of the same subject, though in a somewhat different method. The last-named author has devoted a special work to the grammar of the Mishnah,[5] which had been before treated by L. Dukes and Dr. Geiger, and made a critical edition of the Mekhiltha,[6] a midrashic commentary on Exodus xii. to end, with his own commentary in Hebrew, but without the help of the MSS. of this work existing in Oxford, the British Museum, and the Italian Libraries. The *Tosiftha*, or additions, *i.e.* the Mishnah with some additions according to the redaction of R. Hiyyâ, has been edited within the last few years after a MS. of Vienna. Another older MS. of it was discovered at Erfurt, and a detailed description

---

[1] *Pirke Aboth*, erster Peroq. 8vo. Berlin, 1875.
[2] *Hodegetica in Mishnam*, etc. 8vo. Leipzig, 1867.
[3] *Einleitung in die Mischnah.* 8vo. Frankfort-o.-M., 1876.
[4] *Zur Geschichte der jüdischen Tradition*, 1 Theil. 8vo. Vienna, 1869.
[5] *Studien über die Sprache der Mishna.* 8vo. Vienna, 1867.
[6] *Mechilta*, etc. 8vo. Vienna, 1865.

of it is given by Dr. Zuckermandel.[1] He promises us a newly revised edition of this text. Dr. Dünner, Rabbi at Amsterdam, has published a monograph on the method of this Talmudical book.[2] The Gemara, a kind of commentary on the Mishnah, was composed in both schools, that of Palestine and that of Babylon. The text of the former, of which we possess only four "orders," is in a very bad state, and what makes the matter still worse, mediaeval Jewish schools, having had more reverence for the Gemara of Babylon, neglected almost entirely the study of that of Jerusalem, and consequently no old commentary on it is in existence. The only means therefore, in the absence of old MSS., for establishing a critical text, is to compare passages of this Gemara with similar ones to be found in that of Babylon and in other Talmudical books. This work was begun by the before-mentioned Dr. Frankel, after he had published an introductory treatise on the method of this Gemara,[3] a kind of continuation of his similar work on the Mishnah. To a critical text this lamented writer added a commentary in Hebrew, which is of the highest value;[4] unhappily for this branch of literature he died after having published only half of the first section of this Gemara, leaving three and a half unfinished. Since his death a MS. of the first part of this Gemara, with the commentary of R. Israel Sirilio, has been found in Palestine, and has passed into the hands of Dr. Lehmann, Rabbi at Mayence. A part of it is now being published by him, with the addition of a commentary of his own.[5] We are sorry to say that the variations which this MS. offers are not of great assistance for the establishment of a correct text, and Dr. Lehmann's own production is utterly valueless. This Gemara was probably concluded in the fifth century A.D., consequently it is more than 200 years older than that of Babylon. The learned Rabbi J. Wiesner, however, has

---

[1] See Dr. Berliner's *Magazin*, 1875.
[2] *Die Theorien über Wesen und Ursprung der Tosephtha.* 8vo. Amsterdam, 1874.
[3] *Introductio in Talmud Hierosolymitanum.* 8vo. Berlin, 1870.
[4] *Talmud Hierosol.* ordo *Seraim*, etc. Vol. primum. 4to. Vindobonae, 1874.
[5] *Talmud Jeruschalmi*, etc. Folio. Moguntiae, 1875.

tried to prove in a monograph[1] that it was not composed before 800 A.D., and consequently 100 years later than that of Babylon. If this fact could be proved, it would introduce a great confusion into theories based upon the supposed dates of both Gemaras, but the question is still open to discussion, although we confess for ourselves that Rabbi Wiesner has done much to shake our confidence in the priority of the Jerusalem Gemara over that of Babylon. The latter has been taken in hand by one of the greatest living Talmudists, R. Nathan Rabbinovicz of Munich. He has collated the famous MS. belonging to the Royal Library in this town, and is now publishing the *variae lectiones*[2] of this MS., together with those of the parts existing in MS. in all other libraries of Europe except the Vatican, as well as the readings to be found in old editions and old commentators. Up to the present time six parts only have appeared, and we are afraid it will take more than a lifetime to finish it on the large scale upon which the editor pursues his work. And when it is done, the same process will have to be gone through with the aid of the Vatican MS., which is older than that of Munich. It is therefore to be feared that the present generation will not see the critical text of this Gemara, for the appearance of which Professor Nöldeke expresses so much anxiety in the preface to his grammar of the Mandaic dialect. Commentaries on various parts of this Gemara by R. Hananel of Kairowan (tenth century), which are now in the course of publication,[3] are of great value for settling the text. R. Isaak Lampronti, Rabbi of Ferrara (eighteenth century), composed a kind of concordance to the Talmud, a part of which was published at Venice, but has become out of print. We are glad to mention that the Society for Publication of Hebrew Texts[4] has begun the reprint of this important work, as well as the publication of the inedited part of it. An attempt to compose a grammar of the Babylonian Gemara, viz. of the part

---

[1] *Gib'ath Yerushalaim*. 8vo. Wien, 1872. (Extract from the hash-*Shahar*).
[2] *Variae lectiones in Mischnam et in Talmud Babylonicum*. Monachii, 1867 seqq.
[3] On the part *Pesahim*. 8vo. Paris, 1868.
[4] *Pahad Yizhaq*. Lyck, 1868 seqq.

which is not written in pure Hebrew, nor in the Aramaic dialect of Palestine, has been successfully made in Italian by the late Professor Luzzatto;[1] this grammar has now been translated into German by Dr. Krüger,[2] who has added a few notes to it. Dr. Nöldeke has sufficiently proved that this idiom is almost identical with that of the books of the Mandaites.[3] The lexicographical study of this Gemara has been in the last few years much advanced by Dr. Perles,[4] H. Schorr,[5] and Dr. Kohut;[6] by the two latter chiefly by the examination of Persian words and ideas. Buxtorf's Talmudical lexicon has been re-edited by Dr. Fischer:[7] many additions were supplied by Dr. Fleischer at the beginning of the work; those of the late Dr. Fürst are seldom based on the solid ground of modern philological research. A most valuable contribution to the lexicography of the Talmud will be M. Levy's dictionary,[8] to which Dr. Fleischer regularly contributes: it has now reached the letter *gimmel*. As to the Midrash, a kind of popular interpretation or homilies on the Holy Scriptures, we have to mention the *Pesiqtha* of R. Kahana, published after MSS., with an able commentary in Hebrew, by M. S. Buber.[9] We do not, however, agree with his opinion when he takes this Midrash to be the oldest Agadic book. The book *Vehazahir*, a kind of Midrash on Exodus and Numbers, the first part of which has been published by Dr. Freimann,[10] after an unique MS. at Munich, was certainly not composed in the eighth or ninth century A.D., as the editor imagines; it is probably a compilation made in France in the twelfth century. Let us conclude with the fifth volume of Dr. Jellinek's col-

---

[1] *Elementi grammaticali del Caldeo biblico e del dialetto talmudico Babilonense.* 8vo. Padova, 1861.
[2] 8vo. Breslau, 1873.
[3] *Mandäische Grammatik.* 8vo. p. xxv. Halle, 1875.
[4] *Grätz Monatsschrift*, 1870, p. 210 seqq.
[5] *He-Haluz*, vii., viii.
[6] *Abhandlungen der Morgenländischen Gesellschaft*, iv. 3
[7] *Joannis Buxtorfii P. Lexicon*, etc. 4to. Leipzig, 1869 seqq.
[8] *Neuhebräisches und chalduisches Wörterbuch über die Talmudim und Midraschim.* 4to. Leipzig, 1875. 3 fasc.
[9] *Pesikta, redigirt in Palästina*, von R. Kahana. 8vo. Lyck, 1868.
[10] *Wehishir opus continens Midrashim*, etc. 8vo. Lipsiae, 1873.

lection of small Midrashim[1] belonging to various epochs; they fully prove how anxious the Rabbis at all times were to keep up an ethical standard among the Jews by relating to them anecdotes of great men in the form of parables or popular tales. We have no doubt many will ask why have not these books been translated in order to make them accessible to the general public? The answer is that it is impossible for any one man to do so, as these books require a knowledge of various branches of science. And after all a translation of the Gemara, in which everything is highly unmethodical,[2] would be unintelligible, not to speak of discussions on ritual, which cannot be reproduced in a modern language. In order to prove this assertion we refer the curious reader to the French translation of the two Gemaras on Berakhoth by M. Schwab, which has lately appeared.[3] This is a very bad translation, full of errors and mistakes, for the translator, being almost ignorant of the language of the Talmud, could not even understand the persons, mostly Polish Jews and not very good French scholars, who assisted him; still it will be sufficient to show how irregular the composition of the Talmud is, which, in fact, consists of notes taken by pupils and put together without any method whatever. And this may be even seen in Berakhoth, though the clearest of all the tractates composing this vast encyclopaedia. All that, in our opinion, can be done for the Talmud is to treat it as an encyclopaedia, to take it to pieces and analyze the statements made on various subjects. This method has been followed in our present time. Dr. Levysohn has given an account of the Zoology of the Talmud,[4] R. J. Wiesner is preparing a similar book on the Botany,[5] Dr. Graetz[6] and M. Derenbourg[7] have done

[1] *Bet ha-Midrasch*, 5ter Theil. 8vo. Wien, 1873
[2] *e.g.* we may find after a question or rite an astronomical rule, followed immediately by a lexicographical explanation of some dialectical expression, next to which may come a legendary history, with a geographical statement after it, etc.
[3] *Traité des Berakhoth*, etc. 8vo. Paris, 1871.
[4] *Die Zoologie des Talmud*. 8vo. Frankfort-o.-M., 1858.
[5] See Dr. Berliner's *Magazin*, 1875.
[6] *Geschichte der Juden*, third and fourth volumes.
[7] *Essai sur l'histoire et la géographie de la Palestine*, 1ère partie. 8vo. Paris, 1867.

the same for historical subjects, and the present writer for the geographical part.[1] We have already mentioned treatises on the philology of the Talmud; the subjects of Medicine,[2] Law,[3] and Ethics[4] have had their investigators more than twenty years ago, but the work was not pursued with strict method. A kind of general encyclopaedia of the Talmud is in the course of publication;[5] the author of it is Dr. Hamburger, who is already known by his former publication on Talmudical subjects entitled, 'The spirit of the Agadah.' Let us conclude with Mr. Hershon's book, 'The Pentateuch according to the Talmud,'[6] of which only Genesis is out. The compiler having neglected the Gemara of Jerusalem and the Midrash, his book is incomplete; besides, he quotes the Gemara of Babylon from uncritical editions.

"COMMENTARIES ON THE HOLY SCRIPTURES.—We shall not speak of those composed by Dr. Graetz, the late Professor Luzzatto, and by some other Jews; these belong to the modern school; nor can we enumerate all commentaries of a Rabbinical character by modern authors in Poland or the East, for we have not seen them, and, to speak strictly, they are only *rechauffés* from old Rabbinical writers: the following alone have a right to be mentioned here. Dr. Berliner has published a revised edition of Rashi's commentary on the Pentateuch;[7] we regret to say that the editor had not the best MSS. at his disposal. Abraham Ibn Ezra is one of the most acute commentators, and not always easily intelligible, because his style is very concise, and he likes to be enigmatical; the more important therefore is it to have a correct critical text of such an author. Dr. Friedländer, who has brought out for the Hebrew Literature Society in London an English translation of Ibn Ezra's commentary on Isaiah, is about to publish the Hebrew text of it collated with all known MSS. Ibn Ezra usually

---

[1] *La géographie du Talmud.* 8vo. Paris, 1868.
[2] By Wunderbar.
[3] By the late Dr. Fassel.
[4] By Dukes, Benamoseg, and others.
[5] *Realencyclopaedie für Bibel und Talmud.* 1st fasc. 8vo. Leipzig, 1869.
[6] 8vo. London, 1872.
[7] *Raschii in Pentateuchum commentarius*, etc. 8vo. Berol., 1866.

made two redactions of his commentaries: those on Exodus and Esther appeared a long time ago; the latter has been re-edited from a better MS. Mr. H. J. Mathews,[1] of Exeter College, Oxford, has published the first redaction of the commentary on Canticles, with an English translation, and is preparing that of the shorter redaction on Daniel. A catena of Jewish commentaries in various languages on Isaiah lii. 13 to liv. has been worked up at the request of Dr. Pusey by the present writer, in two volumes; the second of these will contain an English translation.[2] In this translation Mr. Driver, Fellow of New College, has taken a great part; to him we are indebted also for an edition of the commentaries on Jeremiah and Ezekiel by R. Moses ben Shesheth,[3] from an Oxford MS., with an English translation. We understand that Dr. Schiller-Szinessy, of Cambridge, has made great progress with preparing a critical edition of R. David Kimhi's commentary on the Psalms. Great attention was paid to the Book of Job by the late Dr. Israel Schwarz. He added to his own German translation and Hebrew commentary those of R. Isaiah of Trani, Joseph and David Kimhi, and R. Zerahyah of Barcelona.[4] A second part, if the author had not been taken away by a premature death, would have contained R. Saadyah Gaon's and Moses Jikatilia's oommentaries in Arabic, with a critical introduction by the editor. Mr. Nutt, Sub-librarian of the Bodleian Library, is about to publish a commentary on Isaiah by R. Eliezer of Beaugenci. R. Kirchheim, of Frankfort-on-the-Main, has brought out a commentary on Chronicles[5] from three MSS., in one of which it is attributed to Abraham Ibn Ezra; the editor refers it to the school or the pupils of the

---

[1] *Commentary on Canticles after the first recension.* 8vo. London, 1874.
[2] *The Fifty-third Chapter of Isaiah according to Jewish Interpreters.* 2 vols. 8vo. Oxford, 1876.
[3] *R. Moses ben Shesheth's Commentary*, etc. 8vo. London, 1871.
[4] *Tikwath Enosch*, etc. tom. i. 8vo. Berol., 1868. The commentary on Proverbs by the same R. Zerahyah has been published by the same editor under the title of *Jmré Noasch.* 8vo. Vienna, 1871.
[5] *Ein Commentar zur Chronik aus dem X^{ten} Jahrhundert.* 8vo. Frankfort-on-the-Main, 1874.

before-mentioned R. Saadyah Gaon. According to our own opinion this commentary was composed in France in the twelfth century. In any case the commentary is of great value for interpretation, as well as for many various readings of the biblical text. Finally, the Society of the *Meqizé Nirdamim* has published Moses Ibn Tibbon's commentary on Canticles and the beginning of Naphthali Wessely's commentary on the Pentateuch.[1] To this department belongs also the anonymous commentary by a rabbi of Provence (? end of thirteenth or beginning of fourteenth century) on the Chaldee translation of the Pentateuch by Onqelos, edited by the Chief Rabbi Dr. N. Adler from an Oxford MS., collated with another at Parma. Commentaries on the Targum are few, and this one is of value for various readings of the text which it contains. To this Dr. Adler has added his own commentary on the Targum, with an elaborate introduction on Onqelos.[2]

"GRAMMAR AND LEXICOGRAPHY.—Before any attempt was made to compose grammatical works, the various Jewish schools, probably about the fifth century, fixed the text of the Holy Scriptures by oral tradition or *Massorah*. Of course the Massorah, as now found in editions of the Bible, is a compilation of a later period, which embodies most former treatises on the subject. A careful edition of it, collated with the best MSS., is desirable. This we are glad to say will be supplied by Herr Frensdorff's Massorah in alphabetical order, the first part of which is already out,[3] and by the complete edition of the Massorah, which is being prepared by Dr. Ginsburg, to whom we are already indebted for his editions of the Masoretical treatises of Jacob ben Hayyim[4] and Elias Levita.[5] Norzi's introduction to his Masoretical commentary on the Holy Scriptures, printed at Venice in 1819, has become as rare as a MS., and scholars

---

[1] Both 8vo. Lyck, 1875.
[2] *Pathshegen* and *Nethinah lagger*, both published in the Pentateuch edition of Wilna, 1874.
[3] *Die Grosse Massorah*. 4to. Leipzig, 1876.
[4] *Jacob ben Chajim's introduction to the Rabbinical Bible*. 8vo. London, 1865.
[5] *Sepher Massoreh ham-Massoreth*, with critical and explanatory notes. 8vo. London, 1867.

must be thankful to Dr. Jellinek for his edition of this interesting introduction, revised after a MS. in an Italian library.[1] The Targum of Onqelos had also its Massorah, which was known by quotations in Levita's works; we know now of an earlier authority who made use of such a Massorah, viz. the anonymous commentator on Onqelos mentioned above. The late Professor Luzzatto found a fragment of it, which he published in a Hebrew periodical. Dr. Berliner discovered the complete work at Parma, and the first part of it is now lying in print before us.[2] The first Hebrew grammarians, such as R. Saadyah Gaon and the Karaitic David, ben Abraham, adopted in the infancy of their grammatical knowledge uniliteral roots; more advanced grammarians, such as Menahem and Dunash, rejected this notion, and kept to biliteral roots, differing in other respects from each other, and thus causing vehement discussions amongst their pupils. Sal. Stern, of Vienna, has published a collection of them from a MS. at Parma.[3] It was only when R. Jehudah Hayyuj became acquainted with the triliteral system of the Arabic grammarians that it was applied by him to Hebrew verbs. His book on the subject was originally written in Arabic, and still exists in MS. in the Bodleian Library. In order to make it accessible to the Jews of all countries, it was translated into Hebrew by Abraham Ibn Ezra and by Moses Jikatilia. The former was brought out by L. Dukes from an incomplete MS., and the latter, which has many additions by the translator, by Mr. Nutt, of the Bodleian, accompanied with an English translation.[4] This book was commented on by the famous R. Jonah Ibn Janâh of Cordova; his opuscula, except one which is lost, will appear shortly in Arabic, with a French translation by MM. Derenbourg, father and son.[5] Somewhat later R. Jonah

---

[1] *Norzi Jed. Sal., Einleitung, Titelblatt und Schlusswort zu seinem massoretischen Bibelcommentar, nach einer italienischen Hschr.* 8vo. Wien, 1876.
[2] *Die Massorah zum Targum Onkelos.* 4to. Berlin, 1875.
[3] *Liber Responsionum.* 8vo. Vindobonae, 1870.
[4] *Two Treatises on Verbs containing feeble and double letters,* etc. 8vo. London, 1870.
[5] *Opuscules et traités d'Abou'l-Walid,* etc. 8vo. Paris, 1876.

composed an elaborate grammar and dictionary of the Hebrew language of his own, both written in Arabic, and afterwards translated into Hebrew by R. Jehudah Ibn Tibbon. The grammar has been published in Hebrew and the dictionary in Arabic.[1] A grammatical treatise composed in Yemen, and more original in its style than in its grammatical knowledge, has been brought out in the Journal Asiatique of Paris by M. J. Derenbourg.[2] We may also mention the new edition of Ben Zeéb's grammar, with a commentary by A. Lebenson.[3]

"POETRY.—The famous poet and philosopher Salomon ben Gabirol still remains the property of Senior Sachs. It will not be an exaggeration to say that nobody can understand this pious and melancholy poet like him. He has lived with him and in him for the last thirty years, and consequently thinks like him. How strange it is that the poet was so much quicker in composing than his friend is in editing and commenting on him! Not more than twenty of his poems have been published by Sachs.[4] Shall we ever see more? The late Dr. Geiger wrote an able monograph in German on this poet.[5] Gabirol's successor, Jehudah Hal-Levy, is perhaps better known to the public, having been made popular through Heine. The publication of his poems was undertaken by the late Professor Luzzatto,[6] but to our very great regret was not continued by him. The Bodleian possesses two copies of his Diwân; would that any one could be found to continue what Luzzatto so ably began! Such a publication would do credit to the Hebrew Literature Society in London. Professor Benedetti, of Pisa,[7] has given an Italian translation of many of Jehudah Hal-Levy's poems, with an able introduction on the poet. This was done also in another way by Dr. Geiger some twenty years ago. About a century after this poet Spain produced

---

[1] *The Book of Hebrew Roots.* 4to. Oxford, 1875.
[2] *Manuel du lecteur*, Journal Asiatique, 1870, t. xvi., p. 309 seqq.
[3] *Talmud lashon 'Ibrith.* 8vo. Wilna, 1874.
[4] *Shir hash-Shirim*, etc. 8vo. Paris, 1868.
[5] *Salomo Gabirol und seine Dichtungen.* 8vo. Leipzig, 1867.
[6] *Diwân*, etc. 8vo. Lyck, 1864.
[7] *Canzoniere sacro di Giuda Levita.* 4to. Pisa, 1871.

another famous poet, known as R. Jehudah el-Harizi. His first attempt was the translation, rather a free one, of Hariri's Maqamas: a part of it, as much as the MS. contains, has been brought out by Professor Chenery,[1] of Oxford, with prefaces of his own, both in Hebrew and in English. Dr. Berliner has brought out a drama composed by R. Moses Zakkuth,[2] after three MSS. This Rabbi is certainly more kabbalist than poet. We pass over in silence the productions of modern poets, who are rather rhymers than poets.

"PHILOSOPHY.—Not much has been published in this branch since the appearance of Munk's edition of Maimonides' *Moreh han-Nebhukhim.*'[3] Dr. P. Frankl printed a paper in the Transactions of the Academy of Vienna on the *Calâm*,[4] a kind of scholastic theology amongst the early Mahomedans; a method applied to biblical passages by the Karaitic philosophers. This was intended to be a preliminary essay to his edition of the philosophical books of the early Karaites. We find in the same Transactions an able paper on Bahya's theologico-philosophical system by Dr. Kaufmann.[5] Professor Fausto Lasinio at Florence has given us the Hebrew translation of Averroes' commentary on Aristotle's Poetics, by Todros Todrosi,[6] and Dr. Herez has published the Hebrew translation of Averroes on the conjunction of the separate intellect with man by Samuel Ibn Tibbon.[7] Dr. Rosin, professor at the Rabbinical school of Breslau, who brought out in 1865 a very elaborate monograph on a commentary on the 613 precepts attributed to the Provençal Rabbi, Aaron Hal-Levi,[8] has just published another exhaustive book on the Ethics of Maimonides, with an historical sketch of Jewish writings on the same subject before Maimonides.[9]

---

[1] *Machbereth Ithiel.* 8vo. London, 1872.
[2] *Yessod Olam.* 8vo. Berlin, 1874.
[3] *Guide des Egarés.* 3 vols. 8vo. Paris, 1866.
[4] *Wiener Sitzungsberichte* (Hist. Philos. Abth.), 1872.
[5] Ibidem, 1874.
[6] Transactions of the University of Pisa, 1873.
[7] *Die Abhandlungen über die Conjunction des separaten Intellects mit dem Menschen*, etc. 8vo. Berlin, 1869.
[8] *Ein Compendium der jüdischen Gesetzkunde aus dem xiv^{ten} Jahrhundert.*
[9] *Die Ethik des Maimonides.* 4to. Breslau, 1876.

Hillel of Verona was one of the best known of the Italian Rabbis, and the edition of his 'Recompenses of the Soul,' made by S. H. Halberstam,[1] is an important contribution to Jewish scholastic philosophy. Finally, a few pages of Jehudah Hal-Levy's philosophico-theological book *Khozri* has been brought out in Arabic, with an English translation, in the miscellaneous volume published by the Hebrew Literature Society as a specimen of a future publication of the whole.[2]

"Of miscellaneous texts we shall only mention one of Abraham Ibn Ezra's astronomical treatises edited by S. H. Halberstam,[3] the *dialoghi d'amore* of Jehudah Abarbanel in Hebrew,[4] the controversial treatises of R. Jehiel of Paris, re-edited by Dr. Grünbaum,[5] and of Isaak Troki by David Deutsch,[6] the second volume of R. Jacob Saphir's Travels in the East,[7] and Gottlober's History of the Kabbalah in Hebrew;[8] and finally, two biographical works in Hebrew, *a.* on the Rabbis of Cracow,[9] and *b.* on those of Jerusalem.[10] Ignorance of the interpretation of the law was considered amongst the Jews of early time as a sin. The study of the law, say the doctors, ranks above everything. In the post-Talmudical time the Jewish schools devoted their attention from time to time to grammar, lexicography, philosophy, and natural science, as we have seen in the course of this report. Dr. Güdemann[11] has undertaken the history of the way in which Jewish schools have pursued these various branches in different countries; the first part, which has just appeared, treats of the Spanish-Arabic school.

"After this brief account of Rabbinical productions which have appeared in the short time of ten years, was not Mr. Cheyne right when he stated in his report of last year, 'The industry of the Jewish scholars is beyond

---

[1] *Tagmulé han-Nephesh.* 8vo. Lyck, 1875.
[2] We have to mention a second edition of Dr. *C*assel's *G*erman translation of this work after the Hebrew text. 8vo. Berlin, 1869.
[3] *Sepher ha-'Ibbur.* 8vo. Lyck, 1874. [4] Ibidem. 8vo. 1874.
[5] *Wikkuach.* 8vo. Thorn, 1873. [6] *Hizzuk Emunah.* 8vo. Berlin, 1873.
[7] *Eben Sappir.* 8vo. Mayence, 1873. [8] 8vo. Wilna, 1869.
[9] '*Ir haz-Zedeq.* 8vo. Cracow, 1869. [10] *Eben Sh'muel.* Wilna, 1874.
[11] *Das jüdische Unterrichtswesen während der Spanisch-Arabischen Periode.* 8vo. Wien, 1873.

all praise'? We might have added, 'and has always been so:' to prove this we have only to give the following account of the number of MSS. still in existence, besides those which were destroyed in various countries by the Crusaders and the Inquisition. Thus the Bodleian Library possesses 2500 MSS.; the British Museum about 750; the Cambridge University Library more than 400; the various Colleges, together with the Beth ham-Midrash in London, about 200; the National Library in Paris 1312; the Royal Library at Munich 413; the libraries of Vienna and Berlin each above 100 MSS.; Parma about 1400; the Vatican above 500; the convent libraries, together with minor ones in Italy, more than 200; St. Petersburg about 1000, chiefly Karaitic MSS; Spain and Portugal together only 100. Of private libraries, the richest seems to be that of the late Firkovitz, which we mentioned above; Baron Günzburg, in Paris, possesses nearly 900 MSS.; and S. H. Halberstam at Bielitz (Austria), more than 300. There are others in the possession of Drs. Zunz and Steinschneider, of O. H. Schorr, of Brody, not to count those which belonged to Luzzatto and Carmoly, and those still hidden in various towns of the East.

"The history of Karaitic literature, derived from the latest acquisitions at St. Petersburg, has been given by Dr. Graetz,[1] the late Dr. Fürst,[2] and by the present writer in German;[3] by the late Prof. Pinsker[4] and B. Gottlober[5] in Hebrew. Magister Gurland has brought out some small Karaite treatises, and especially some travels to Palestine in the sixteenth century.[6] No doubt many publications are issued at Eupatoria, the Leipzig of the Jewish Crimea, but they do not reach our country; perhaps we do not lose much by their absence.

"In Samaritan literature Mr. Nutt gave a full account of

---

[1] *Geschichte der Juden*, tomes v. and vi.
[2] *Geschichte des Karäerthums.* 3 vols. 8vo. Leipzig, 1869.
[3] See above, p. 8, note 1.
[4] *Liqqûtê Qadmoniyyoth.* 8vo. Wien, 1860.
[5] *Kritische Untersuchung über die Geschichte der Karäer.* 8vo. Vilna, 1865.
[6] *Reisebeschreibungen*, etc. 8vo. Lyck, 1865.

it, such as it is, in 1874;[1] since then we have only to add a complete edition of the Samaritan Targum in Hebrew characters by Dr. A. Brüll, with an appendix on Mr. Nutt's book, and the first part of Dr. Harkavy's Catalogue of the Samaritan MSS. at St. Petersburg, written in Russian. Finally, Dr. Kohn, who is well known by his articles on the Samaritan Targum, has just published in the Transactions of the German Oriental Society *Contributions to the Language, Literature, and the Dogma of the Samaritans*.[2] It is to be regretted that the learned author was not acquainted with Mr. Nutt's above-mentioned book before his own had already left the press. He promises, however, to pay full attention to it on a future occasion. J. Reifmann[3] compares the translation of the Pentateuch according to the Samaritans, with the Rabbanite Targums and the Midrashic exposition. The part on Genesis is out, in which the author gives some remarkable indications of the extent to which the former borrowed their interpretations from the latter. Had the author possessed a good library, he could have done much more, but he is unfortunately obliged to live in a small and isolated Polish village, where he is not in a position to enjoy this advantage."

[1] *Fragments of Samaritan Targum, with an introduction*, etc. 8vo. London, 1874.
[2] *Zur Sprache, Literatur und Dogmatik der Samaritaner*, 3 Abhandlungen. 8vo. Leipzig, 1876.
[3] *Sedeh Aram.* 8vo. Berlin, 1875.

HEREFORD:
PRINTED BY AUSTIN AND SONS.

University of California
SOUTHERN REGIONAL LIBRARY FACILITY
405 Hilgard Avenue, Los Angeles, CA 90024-1388
Return this material to the library
from which it was borrowed.

JUL 15 1997

CPSIA information can be obtained
at www.ICGtesting.com
Printed in the USA
LVHW081452211118
597922LV00010B/771/P